SIMONE BILES

SIMONE BILES

GREATEST OF ALL TIME

HEATHER E. SCHWARTZ

LERNER PUBLICATIONS ◆ MINNEAPOLIS

Lerner Publications Company
An imprint of Lerner Publishing Group, Inc.
241 First Avenue North
Minneapolis, MN 55401 USA

For reading levels and more information, look up this title at www.lernerbooks.com.

The images in this book are used with the permission of: Laurence Griffiths/Getty Images, pp. 2, 36, 38; Jamie Squire/Getty Images, pp. 6–7, 29–31, 35; Xavier Laine/Getty Images, pp. 8, 39; Jeremy Woodhouse/Getty Images, p. 9; Maddie Meyer/Getty Images, p. 11; AP Photo/Melissa J. Perenson/CSM, pp. 12, 25; Bob Levey/Stringer/Getty Images, p. 13; Gerlach Delissen/Corbis/Getty Images, p. 14; Ian MacNicol/Stringer/Getty Images, p. 16; Julian Finney/Getty Images, p. 17; Alex Livesey/Stringer/Getty Images, p. 18; Pascal Le Segretain/Getty Images, p. 19; Harry How/Getty Images, p. 20; John Lamparski/Getty Images, p. 22; Bruce Glikas/FilmMagic/Getty Images, p. 23; AP Photo/Vadim Ghirda, p. 24; Kyodo News/Getty Images, p. 27; Ulrik Pedersen/NurPhoto/Getty Images, p. 28; Justin Sullivan/Getty Images, p. 33; Gabriela Maj/Stringer/Getty Images, p. 34; The Asahi Shimbun/Getty Images, p. 37; Saul Loeb/Pool/Getty Images, p. 40; Katharine Lotze/Getty Images, p. 41.

Cover: Kyle Okita/CSM/Shutterstock.

Main body text set in Rotis Serif Std 55 Regular. Typeface provided by Adobe Systems.

Editor: Lauren Foley **Designer:** Connie Kuhnz

Library of Congress Cataloging-in-Publication Data

Names: Schwartz, Heather E., author.
Title: Simone Biles : greatest of all time / Heather E. Schwartz.
Description: Minneapolis, MN: Lerner Publications, [2023] | Series: Gateway Biographies | Includes bibliographical references and index. | Audience: Ages 9–14 years | Audience: Grades 4–6 | Summary: "Two-time Olympic gymnast Simone Biles reigns over gymnastics. With four impressive skills already named after her, Biles has amassed legions of fans. Explore this standout superstar's career and life"—Provided by publisher.
Identifiers: LCCN 2021063019 (print) | LCCN 2021063020 (ebook) | ISBN 9781728458489 (library binding) | ISBN 9781728463261 (paperback) | ISBN 9781728461311 (ebook)
Subjects: LCSH: Biles, Simone, 1997– –Juvenile literature. | Women gymnasts–United States–Biography–Juvenile literature. | Gymnasts–United States–Biography–Juvenile literature. | African American women Olympic athletes–Biography–Juvenile literature.
Classification: LCC GV460.2.B55 S36 2023 (print) | LCC GV460.2.B55 (ebook) | DDC 796.44092 [B]–dc23/eng/20220204

LC record available at https://lccn.loc.gov/2021063019
LC ebook record available at https://lccn.loc.gov/2021063020

Manufactured in the United States of America
4-1009410-50214-6/2/2023

TABLE OF CONTENTS

Biles flips on the balance beam during the Tokyo Olympics Finals.

The world watched as Simone Biles mounted the balance beam at the 2021 Tokyo Olympics. She'd made the difficult decision to pull out of several Olympic event finals, such as the team final and the individual all-around. Some criticized her for withdrawing from the events, but her fans understood and supported her. The pressure was on, and no one's opinions mattered but her own. Biles had to focus. She was the greatest gymnast of all time, and she was getting back in the game.

Her moves were graceful and strong as she moved through her routine of back handsprings, flips, and split leaps. She knew her score would decrease due to a last-minute change she'd made to her dismount. Without any twists, her dismount was going to be easier than planned. But she was OK with that. She was determined to take care of herself even if it meant losing points.

Biles's coach Cecile Landi (*left*) congratulates Biles after the balance beam event.

After soaring through the air in a double backflip, she stuck the landing and raised her arms with a huge smile on her face. As she left the mat, she touched her chest with relief. She ran to hug her coach.

Biles had done it. She'd come back from one of the most difficult challenges she'd ever faced as a gymnast. Not only had she proven herself physically, but she had just shown the world how important it was to consider mental health. "I think it [mental health] should be talked about a lot more, especially with athletes," she said. "At the end of the day, we're not just entertainment—we're humans."

Getting Started

Born on March 14, 1997, in Columbus, Ohio, Simone Biles started life sometimes feeling hungry and scared. Her mother struggled with substance abuse and was in and out of jail. There wasn't always enough to eat for Simone; her younger sister, Adria; and her two older siblings, Tevin and Ashley. Simone's father was absent. Often no adult was at home to properly care for the kids.

When Simone was three, she was placed in foster care. She spent a few years in and out of foster homes, and she was excited whenever she got to visit her grandparents Ron and Nellie Biles. When Simone was six, Ron and Nellie adopted her and Adria. Another family member adopted Tevin and Ashley.

The suburb where Biles grew up is near Houston, Texas (*above*).

Growing up in Spring, Texas, Simone eventually started calling her grandparents Mom and Dad. Ron and Nellie supported Simone from the beginning. They taught her how to treat other people well. Simone was grateful for the example they set.

Simone's parents gave her a loving, stable home where she felt safe and supported. Like many children, she loved jumping and tumbling from an early age. She was six when her day-care class took a field trip to Bannon's Gymnastix. She saw gymnasts practicing their routines at the gym. She was so inspired that she started copying their moves right there.

Soon after, her parents received a note from a gymnastics coach at the gym. The coach had noticed Simone and suggested that she start practicing at the gym. Simone's parents thought it was a great idea, so she started training there. She was only doing it for fun, but coaches couldn't help noticing she was unusually strong for a six-year-

Early Diagnosis

Simone had plenty of energy for training in gymnastics. But that energy caused some problems when she had to sit still in school. At an early age, she was diagnosed with attention deficit hyperactivity disorder (ADHD). She started taking medication that helped her concentrate, whether she was working on school assignments or training at the gym.

Biles (*right*) talks with Aimee Boorman before a competition.

old. She surprised everyone when she climbed a rope all the way to the gym's ceiling. By the time she was eight, Simone was being coached by Aimee Boorman. Boorman believed in Simone's potential to become an elite athlete.

Boorman had never trained an elite athlete before, and Simone hadn't worked toward a goal that big either. But they were prepared to go on the journey together. And Boorman focused on making sure Simone had fun. She let Simone try new skills whether they'd help her win in competition or not. She also made sure Simone had time off with friends and family to enjoy being a kid.

At 10, Simone was competing against top gymnasts of the same age from around the country. In 2010 she competed at the Women's Junior Olympic National Championships, the highest competition below the elite level. She won a gold medal in the floor exercise and a bronze medal on the vault. She competed at the 2011

American Classic in Houston, Texas, her first meet at the elite level. She placed third in the all-around event, and she won first place on balance beam and vault.

Simone's skill at the elite level was impressive. Soon it was time to choose what she wanted to do for the rest of her life. If she intended to reach the top heights of success in her sport, she'd need to train harder and more seriously than she already was training.

Training for Success

When Biles is training, her schedule is full. She spends over 30 hours each week training in the gym. Stretching her muscles helps prevent injury and is a big part of her daily workout. It also allows Simone's arms and legs to reach the extreme positions her routines call for. She spends some of her time practicing basic skills, like flips and spins. And she also does cardio training to stay in shape and maintain her stamina.

Giving Her All

By 14, Simone knew what she wanted to do. She left public school and began homeschooling so she could train for six to eight hours at the gym each day. At each session, she stretched her muscles and practiced basic skills. Cardio was a part of her training too.

Simone had to give up school dances and other activities many other teenagers do. At times she was lonely. But she had her parents, sister, and four German shepherds to keep her company. In many ways, her life was normal. She still enjoyed watching *Pretty Little Liars* on TV, reading *The Hunger Games* books, and eating at one of her favorite restaurants, Olive Garden. And spending most of her time in the gym wasn't all about sacrifice. Simone made new friends at the gym, and she loved her sport.

When Simone dove into gymnastics full-time, there was no stopping her. Once a month, she worked with renowned coach Marta Karolyi, who trained gymnasts at Karolyi Ranch in Houston, Texas. Karolyi's methods were different from Boorman's. Karolyi taught Simone not to

Marta Karolyi (*right*) and her husband, Bela, at Karolyi Ranch in 2011

Biles competing in the all-around final of the 2013 Gymnastics World Championships

cheer for other gymnasts and not to laugh, both of which might show she was having too much fun and not taking training seriously. While Simone wanted to succeed in her sport, she felt these conditions went too far. She told Karolyi that she'd perform better if she could still be herself.

Karolyi also pushed Simone to try a difficult move on vault, the Amanar. It felt more dangerous than challenging to the young gymnast. Simone had to stand up for herself again. She told Karolyi she wouldn't perform the move. "I knew that I wasn't ready for it. You have to trust your body, your instincts. And you also have to protect yourself," she later said.

By the time Simone competed at the 2012 US Classic, she was ready. She'd gradually worked up to the move and felt confident about performing it after practicing it in training. Her hard work and determination paid off. She performed the Amanar and won the junior competition. Then at her first world gymnastics championship as a senior competitor in 2013, she was crowned the all-around world champion, becoming the first Black woman ever to win the title.

In 2014 Simone's parents showed their support for their daughter in a big way. They built the World Champions Centre in Spring, Texas. The gym provided a safe place for gymnastics and children's tumbling training. Simone's longtime coach, Boorman, helped establish the gym. Then Simone had her own home base for training.

The gym would eventually open to the public. It meant a lot to Simone to show other Black athletes a path to success in gymnastics. "Representation matters, and we want to inspire the next generation to pursue their passion," Simone said. "Kids can come in and we will be training in the back, and they can see we are just like them. It helps them understand they can do it too."

Creating New Moves

In 2013 Simone's lower leg was sore after she landed a certain way. She and Boorman came up with a new way to land. The new way felt better, but it wasn't easy. The landing made it into the official gymnastics rule book and is known as the Biles.

Biles soars over the beam during the 2015 Gymnastics World Championships.

Simone won the all-around world championship for the second time in 2014. In 2015 she decided to turn professional. As a professional, she wouldn't be allowed to compete for a college team. She gave up her dream of attending the University of California, Los Angeles (UCLA), and signed with the athletics brand Nike. She started to make money through sponsorships.

Later that year, Biles won the all-around world championship for the third year in a row, becoming the first woman to win the world title three straight times. She won several more awards that year too, for a career total of 14 world championship medals. That was more than any US gymnast had ever won. And 10 were gold medals—more than any other female gymnast had won.

Even after all her accomplishments, Simone was far from finished. She was just getting started.

Going for Olympic Gold

In 2016 Biles tried out for the US Olympic Gymnastics Team. The competition was fierce. Olympic gold medalists

Biles has fun while performing her floor routine at the 2016 Olympics.

Gabby Douglas and Aly Raisman were there too, along with many other exceptional gymnasts. But Biles didn't let the stress get to her. "I think we all thought we would be a little bit more nervous in the waiting room, but we were just . . . kind of having fun because you want to remember it as having fun instead of almost passing out," Biles said.

When she won the all-around, she knew she would automatically make the team. She also won the floor exercise and vault. She took fourth on balance beam and tied for fourth on uneven bars.

No one was surprised that Biles was going to the Olympics. She was considered a favorite to win gold in

Biles (*right*) and Raisman show off their 2016 Olympic medals.

Rio de Janeiro, Brazil. Fans hoped she would help the team take five medals for floor, vault, balance beam, all-around, and team. But Biles wasn't interested in letting the world's expectations throw her off-balance. Instead, she focused on her teammates. She was excited to spend time with them and glad they could all lean on one another for support during the competition.

Millions watched as Biles and the rest of the team competed in the 2016 Olympic Games. They cheered as Biles leaped and soared during the floor exercise. She received the top score and won gold in the event.

Tiny Champion

Biles is 4 feet 8 (1.4 m), and she's always made the most of her short stature. In gymnastics, being short can help athletes perform better spins and flips. In 2016 she was the shortest

member of Team USA. She got to carry the American flag at the closing ceremony of the Olympic Games. The flagpole was almost twice her height. She also took some fun photos for fans, posing with exceptionally tall athletes like swimming champion Michael Phelps, who is 6 feet 4 (1.9 m).

Biles (*left*) and the rest of Team USA smile during an interview after the 2016 Olympics.

The score helped her become the Olympic all-around champion. She also won a gold medal on the vault and a bronze medal on balance beam. Team USA took an all-around gold medal too.

All of her wins at the Games were incredible accomplishments. The media called Biles an Olympic superstar and the golden girl of the Olympics. Reporters asked her what she'd say to kids who looked up to her and hoped to be Olympians too. "I would just tell them to always work hard and have fun in what you do, because I think that's when you're more successful," Biles said. "You have to choose to do it and not [have] anybody else telling you [that] you have to do it."

After months of training and competing together, Biles and her teammates got to stay together for a bit longer. They joined the Kellogg's Tour of Gymnastics Champions.

The tour visited 36 cities in the United States, bringing world-class gymnastics to fans. Fans were especially eager to know what Biles had planned next. They hoped she'd be back for the 2020 Olympic Games in Tokyo.

Taking a Break

In September 2016 the media broke a story about Biles that had nothing to do with her success as an athlete or plans for the future. Instead, it focused on what should have been private medical records. Russian hackers claimed they had posted Biles's Olympic drug-testing files online. Their website said she had tested positive for a banned substance. But Biles had permission from USA Gymnastics to use the medication, and the organization

Eating Right

For Biles, part of staying healthy is eating healthful and nutritious foods. Her day often begins with oatmeal and water. After training, she'll fuel with a protein shake. Lunch is pasta, chicken, or salmon. But while she eats healthful foods most of the time, sometimes she enjoys sugary snacks. "I do love to snack," she said. "My weakness is cookies or sour candy."

was quick to back her up. They stated that Biles had not broken any rules.

Biles spoke up for herself too. She explained that she has ADHD and has taken medication for it since she was young. She also made clear that she believes fair play is important in gymnastics and that she always follows the rules.

Biles wasn't happy about what the hackers had done because they'd forced her to speak publicly about her medical condition before she was ready to do so. But she'd never tried to hide her ADHD. She'd even written about it in her autobiography, *Courage to Soar: A Body in Motion, a Life in Balance.* It was set to come out just a few months later in November 2016. By speaking up, she became a role model for others with ADHD.

Biles holding her book, *Courage to Soar,* in 2016

After touring with her Olympic teammates, Biles knew she needed a break. In November she announced that she was stepping away from gymnastics. "I'm going to take some time off from the gym, just so that I can go out, have fun and really just embrace the moment that we have," she said. "Especially vacation, because I couldn't do that before with how much I trained. I was always in the gym."

Biles, at 20, had spent many years of her life dedicating all her time to gymnastics. But she had other interests too. As an Olympic champion, she received many exciting opportunities. During her break in 2017, she competed on *Dancing with the Stars* for nine weeks. She made it to the semifinal and took fourth place. She also made a guest appearance on an episode of the NBC show *Little Big Shots: Forever Young*, during which she surprised the world's oldest gymnast, 91-year-old Johanna Quaas. And she took a fun family vacation to Hawaii, where she relaxed on the beach.

Biles (*right*) with *Dancing with the Stars* partner, Sasha Farber

In the summer of 2017, Biles decided she was ready to get back in the gym. She was eager to compete again, but she focused on taking her training day by day.

Telling Her Story

By late 2017, Biles's former coach, Boorman, had found a new job in Florida. But Biles didn't want to return to the pressures she'd experienced working with Karolyi. She started working with two new coaches, Cecile and Laurent Landi. They pushed her to do more difficult moves but also offered a collaborative approach and support. Biles was excited to work with them.

Soon she needed their understanding and support more than she'd ever imagined. Several gymnasts had publicly reported that Larry Nassar, the USA Gymnastics team doctor, had abused them. One day, Biles broke down crying. She told the Landis that Nassar had abused her too.

Biles (*right*) high-fives Laurent Landi in 2018. Cecile and Laurent supported Biles in and out of the gym when she decided to tell her story.

Biles (*bottom*) stretches with Cecile Landi's help.

After that, Biles sometimes fell apart at the gym. Gymnastics didn't always feel like a safe place anymore. She cried often and couldn't always stay to train. The Landis and Biles's parents were there for her, encouraging her to take the mental breaks she needed.

Biles was a champion in her sport, and her voice had power. Her coaches encouraged her to use it. Soon Biles was ready. In 2018 she went on Twitter to stand by her fellow teammates and friends and to stand up for herself. "For far too long I've asked myself 'Was I too naive? Was it my fault?' I now know the answer to those questions. No. No. It was not my fault. No, I will not and should not carry the guilt that belongs to Larry Nassar, USAG [USA Gymnastics], and others," she wrote. "After hearing the brave stories of my friends and other survivors, I know that this horrific experience does not define me."

Biles chose not to speak at Nassar's trial. She was training hard. She'd only recently felt brave enough to tell people what had happened to her. And she hadn't had time to process the abuse with a therapist. She knew she needed to protect her mental health. But her words made a big impact, adding another voice to the more than 150 women who accused Nassar of abuse. The judge sentenced Nassar to 40 to 175 years in prison for his crimes.

Meanwhile, Biles had much happier events to focus on. *Courage to Soar* was made into a movie that aired on the television network Lifetime. The movie, *The Simone Biles Story: Courage to Soar*, received good reviews. Viewers praised the realistic yet inspirational approach to Biles's story. They enjoyed learning about her personal life as much as about her gymnastics achievements.

Biles also decided to go to college that year. She'd given up her dream of attending college when she had decided to focus on gymnastics. But she was ready to try. She had her eye on UCLA again but didn't know how she could attend classes and train at the same time.

She soon realized there were more options than she'd imagined. She started studying business administration at the University of the People, an online college. Biles loved its flexibility and became an ambassador for the program, speaking about how well it could work for busy students. She even set up the Simone Biles Legacy Scholarship Fund to help other foster children who might need support attending college.

Biles's floor routine won a gold medal at the 2018 Gymnastics World Championships. No one could tell that she had a painful kidney stone.

Coming Back

In July 2018 Biles competed for the first time since the Rio Olympic Games nearly two years earlier. At the US Classic, she felt rusty and made some mistakes. Her landing on vault wasn't great. She fell during her uneven bars routine. But her goal was to do her best, and she earned the highest all-around score to win first place.

Later that year, Biles went to the Gymnastics World Championships. The night before the competition, she was hospitalized for a painful kidney stone. Doctors wanted to prescribe pain medication, but if she took it, she'd go against substance regulations for athletes. She decided to push through the pain.

Determined to do her best, she won gold medals in the floor, vault, all-around final, and team final. She took silver on uneven bars and bronze on beam. She was proud of herself, but people criticized her on Twitter because they wanted her to win gold on beam. Biles admitted that it was hard for her to see all the tweets about how disappointed people were in her and her performance. But for Biles, the expectations she had for herself were more important than what other people thought.

Biles focuses as she swings on the uneven bars.

Biles does the splits over the beam at the 2019 US Gymnastics Championships.

Biles kept training and, in summer 2019, headed to the US Classic again. She'd already proven herself over and over. But she still had goals and always aimed to up her game. "Every year you should try to be better than you were the year before. So it doesn't matter how far ahead I am. I should try to better my gymnastics and myself," she said.

Signature Skills

By the time she was 24, Biles had four gymnastics skills named after her. Two moves, the Biles and Biles 2, are performed in the floor exercise. Two others, both called the Biles, are performed on vault and beam.

Biles arcs around the uneven bars during the 2019 US Gymnastics Championships.

At the competition, Biles once again took first place with the all-around win. From there, she went on to compete in the 2019 US Gymnastics Championships. While performing on the balance beam, she attempted a double-double dismount, a move in which a gymnast flips twice and completes two twists in the air before landing on the mat. Not only was she the first gymnast to attempt it, but she landed it too. After the impressive move, she won gold on balance beam.

Biles wasn't done yet. At the world championship that year, she won five gold medals, including one in the all-around event. She became the first gymnast in over 60 years to win that many medals at one US championship. To top the competition off, she also set a record with her new career total of 25 world championship medals. It was more than any other gymnast had ever won.

Biles was focused and motivated. She was physically and mentally strong. She seemed unstoppable. And the next Olympic Games were on the horizon.

Biles (*center*) celebrates her first place win on the podium.

Cross-Training

Biles sometimes cross-trains. Swimming, running, and biking help her stay in shape. Her schedule might include swimming 2 miles (3.2 km) each week, biking 10 miles (16 km), or running a mile (1.6 km) right before heading to the gym for gymnastics training.

Taking Control

Biles controls how much she trains. She could manage the mental and physical stress that came with performing as a professional athlete. But she could not control the events that took over the world in early 2020. COVID-19 was spreading globally. In March the World Health Organization declared a pandemic. All over the world, businesses and schools shut down. People stayed home and stayed away from others to avoid spreading or catching the deadly disease. The 2020 Olympics were postponed until 2021.

Biles could still go to the gym, but she felt overwhelmed at the thought of training for the Olympics for another year. Her Olympic training schedule was grueling. She was in the gym seven hours a day. She trained once a day on Thursdays and Saturdays. And she had two training sessions on Mondays, Tuesdays, Wednesdays, and Fridays. Her only day off was Sunday.

Life got more difficult when her gym shut down for weeks in 2020. Suddenly, she couldn't train or hang out with her teammates. She had too much time alone, and she began to focus on worries, doubts, and problems.

Biles found herself getting depressed and sleeping a lot. But she took control of her life where she could. When the gym reopened, she got back to training. And in April 2021, she made the decision to leave her longtime sponsor Nike. She wasn't happy with the company's treatment of female athletes. So she would represent Athleta, a women's clothing brand. With Athleta's financial support,

Biles appeared in Athleta ads like this one outside their stores, in commercials, and more.

Maya Angelou wrote the poem that inspired Biles's collarbone tattoo.

she also planned a post-Olympics tour that could draw just as much attention as those traditionally run by USA Gymnastics.

Biles was busy in June. She won her seventh national championship in the first week. Afterward, she got a tattoo on her collarbone. It said, "and still I rise," referencing a Maya Angelou poem about Black pride. "It's a reminder and a tribute to everything I had been through, and that I always come out on top," Biles said.

Because She Could

Heading into the Tokyo Olympics, Biles was performing moves no other gymnast in the world could manage. But even when she completed them skillfully, her scores didn't always reflect the difficulty of the moves. One explanation given for this was that judges didn't want to encourage other gymnasts to attempt moves that may lead to injury. Biles was frustrated to know she was being underscored. But she continued to up the difficulty of her moves for one simple reason: because she could.

Later in the month, *Simone vs Herself* premiered on Facebook Watch. The first episodes in the seven-part series followed Biles as she prepared for the Olympics in Tokyo, Japan. In the documentary, she talked about her life, her career, and the stress from the postponed 2021 Olympics. With the two-part finale set to air a few months later in September, the series would follow her all the way through the Games.

Leaving for the Olympics in Tokyo was hard. Because of the pandemic, Biles's parents couldn't come with her. No crowd would be there to cheer her on. Even though she still had her coaches' support, she felt anxious in a way she hadn't before other competitions. Still, she planned to go ahead with her events.

Biles reaches for the uneven bars during qualifying events at the 2021 Olympics.

Biles leaps through the air at the Tokyo Olympics.

Greatest of All Time

The Tokyo Olympics kicked off with qualifying events.
And Biles knew right away she wasn't performing her best.
Because her anxiety was so high, she was making mistakes.
Her coaches tried to help. They offered pep talks and added
foam pits so she'd know she had a safe cushion if she fell.
But nothing seemed to work. "I was not physically capable
[of performing]," Biles said. "Every avenue we tried, my
body was like, *Simone, chill. Sit down.*"

Thinking she could rely on her training, muscle
memory, and mental strength, Biles pushed on. Then
came the vault event two days later. As Biles launched
herself into the air to perform two and a half twists,

Biles flips over the vault at the Tokyo Olympics.

she realized she was lost in space. She made a snap decision to complete only one and a half. She stumbled as she landed.

The entire experience terrified Biles. She had lost her air awareness and experienced what gymnasts call the twisties. The outcome could have been much worse. "It's so dangerous," she said. "It's basically life or death. It's a miracle I landed on my feet. If that was any other person, they would have gone out on a stretcher."

Biles knew what she had to do. As soon as she landed, she told her coach she was withdrawing from her events at the Olympics. The world was shocked. Critics called her a quitter. They'd expected her to take home five gold medals, and they blamed her for letting them down. But fans recognized the strength and courage it took for Biles to protect her mental and physical health while under so much pressure to compete. They saw her as a role model, especially for athletes and Black people.

For Biles, the decision was the only one she could make. She cheered on her teammates from the sidelines and only returned to the competition to participate in the final balance beam event. Instead of taking home five gold medals as expected, she won a bronze in balance beam and a silver team all-around medal.

Biles (*left*) congratulates 2021 Olympic teammate Suni Lee on her performance.

Soon after the Tokyo Olympics, Biles again showed her strength and courage when she testified against Nassar before the US Senate. She wanted to be sure that everyone knew that the organizations meant to protect her and other athletes had failed. And she didn't pretend it was easy. She was open about the toll it took on her. "Before we entered the room, I was in the back literally bawling my eyes out," she said. "And then, of course, you have to pull yourself together and go out there, be strong for just that moment."

Left to right: Aly Raisman, Simone Biles, McKayla Maroney, and Maggie Nichols at the 2021 US Senate hearing on the FBI mishandling reports of Nassar's abuse

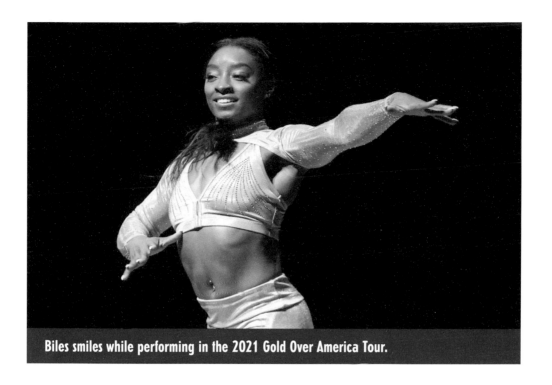
Biles smiles while performing in the 2021 Gold Over America Tour.

It was a difficult year, but by the end of it, Biles was in a much better place. She was attending therapy and back to enjoying gymnastics too. From September through November 2021, she headlined the Gold Over America Tour, traveling the US with an all-star gymnastics team that showcased female athletes in 35 cities. Soon after, all that she'd been through and accomplished was recognized when she was named *Time* magazine's Athlete of the Year.

With the Paris Olympics set for 2024, Biles was considering competing again. But she had time to take a break. More gold medals may be in her future, but Biles's main focus is maintaining her health and happiness.

IMPORTANT DATES

1997   Simone Biles is born on March 14.

2010   Simone wins a gold medal in floor exercise and a bronze medal in vault at the Women's Junior Olympic National Championships.

2013   Simone is the first Black woman to win the all-around world champion title.

2015   Biles turns professional.

2016   Biles wins four gold medals at the Olympics, including one for all-around champion.

Her medical records are hacked, and she speaks out about her ADHD.

2017   Biles takes a break from gymnastics.

She competes on *Dancing with the Stars*.

She appears on the NBC show *Little Big Shots: Forever Young*.

2018   Biles speaks out about being abused by USA
Gymnastics team doctor Larry Nassar.

Her autobiography, *Courage to Soar: A Body in
Motion, a Life in Balance*, is made into a movie.

She starts college at the University of the People.

2020   The Tokyo Olympics are postponed for one year.

2021   *Simone vs Herself,* a new documentary series
about Biles's life, airs on Facebook Watch.

She withdraws from events at the Tokyo Olympics
to protect her mental health.

She returns to the Olympic finals to take bronze
in balance beam and silver in all-around team.

SOURCE NOTES

8 Simone Biles, "Simone Biles Reflects on 'Happy' Bronze Medal after Competing in Women's Beam Final—Tokyo 2020," press conference, courtesy of International Olympic Committee, posted by BeanymanNews, August 3, 2021, YouTube video, 3:14, https://www.youtube.com/watch?v=9Vu8AB-KL80.

14 Emma Brockes, "Simone Biles: 'I Go to Therapy, Because at Times I Didn't Want to Set Foot in the Gym,'" *Guardian* (US edition), March 16, 2019, https://www.theguardian.com /sport/2019/mar/16/simone-biles-therapy-times-didnt-want -set-foot-gym.

15 Bethany Heitman, "How Simone Biles Prioritizes Her Mental Health while Training for the Olympics," *Health*, June 9, 2021, https://www.health.com/celebrities/simone-biles-interview.

18 Brandon Penny, "Simone Biles, Gabby Douglas, Aly Raisman Lead Olympic Women's Gymnastics Team," Team USA, July 10, 2016, https://www.teamusa.org/News/2016/July/10/US-Olympic -Team-Trials-For-Womens-Gymnastics.

20 Simone Biles, "Olympics | Simone Biles Interview on Rio Olympics," interview by Robin Roberts and T.J. Holmes, *Good Morning America*, posted by ABC News, August 19, 2016, YouTube video, 4:46, https://www.youtube.com/watch?v =5wOBzxIm2Fg.

21 Heitman, "Simone Biles Prioritizes Mental Health."

22–23 OlympicTalk, "Simone Clarifies Timeline for Gymnastics Break," NBC Sports, November 18, 2016, https://olympics.nbcsports .com/2016/11/18/simone-biles-gymnastics-break/.

25 Simone Biles (@Simone_Biles), "Feelings . . ." #MeToo, Twitter, January 15, 2018, 3:22 p.m., https://twitter.com/Simone_Biles /status/953014513837715457?ref_src=twsrc%5Etfw%7Ctwcamp %5Etweetembed%7Ctwterm%5E953014513837715457%7Ctwgr% 5E%7Ctwcon%5Es1_&ref_url=https%3A%2F%2Fwww.cnn.com %2F2018%2F01%2F15%2Fus%2Fsimone-biles-larry-nassar %2Findex.html.

29 OlympicTalk, "Simone Biles, Delaying Adulting, Surprises Herself Going into U.S. Classic," NBC Sports, July 19, 2019, https:// olympics.nbcsports.com/2019/07/19/simone-biles-us-classic -gymnastics/.

34 Alice Park and Sean Gregory, "2021 Athlete of the Year: Simone Biles," *Time*, December 9, 2021, https://time.com/athlete-of-the -year-2021-simone-biles/.

37 Carolyn L. Todd, "Here's What Might Have Caused Simone Biles' Dangerous 'Twisties' during the Tokyo Olympics," *Self*, September 27, 2021, https://www.self.com/story/simone-biles -twisties-anxiety-tokyo-olympics.

38 Camonghne Felix, "Simone Biles Chose Herself: 'I Should Have Quit Way before Tokyo," Cut, September 27, 2021, https:// www.thecut.com/article/simone-biles-olympics-2021.html.

40 Felix.

SELECTED BIBLIOGRAPHY

Academy of Achievement. "Simone Biles Biography—Academy of Achievement." Academy of Achievement, last modified September 1, 2021. https://achievement.org/achiever/simone-biles/.

Biles, Simone. "Olympics | Simone Biles Interview on Rio Olympics." Interview by Robin Roberts and T.J. Holmes. *Good Morning America*, posted by ABC News, August 19, 2016. YouTube video, 4:46. https://www.youtube.com/watch?v=5wOBzxIm2Fg.

Biles, Simone. "Simone Biles Reflects on 'Happy' Bronze Medal after Competing in Women's Beam Final—Tokyo 2020." Press conference, courtesy of International Olympic Committee, posted by BeanymanNews, August 3, 2021. YouTube video, 3:14. https://www.youtube.com/watch?v=9Vu8AB-KL80.

Felix, Camonghne. "Simone Biles Chose Herself: 'I Should Have Quit Way before Tokyo." Cut, September 27, 2021. https://www.thecut.com/article/simone-biles-olympics-2021.html.

Heitman, Bethany. "How Simone Biles Prioritizes Her Mental Health while Training for the Olympics." *Health*, June 9, 2021. https://www.health.com/celebrities/simone-biles-interview.

Miller, Korin. "Who Are Simone Biles' Parents? Meet the Supportive Mom and Dad Who Raised the Olympian." *Women's Health*, August 6, 2021. https://www.womenshealthmag.com/life/a37092376/simone-biles-parents/.

OlympicTalk. "Simone Biles, Delaying Adulting, Surprises Herself Going into U.S. Classic." NBC Sports, July 19, 2019. https://olympics.nbcsports.com/2019/07/19/simone-biles-us-classic-gymnastics/.

Park, Alice, and Sean Gregory. "2021 Athlete of the Year: Simone Biles." *Time*, December 9, 2021. https://time.com/athlete-of-the-year-2021-simone-biles/.

Penny, Brandon. "Simone Biles, Gabby Douglas, Aly Raisman Lead Olympic Women's Gymnastics Team." Team USA, July 10, 2016. https://www.teamusa.org/News/2016/July/10/US-Olympic-Team -Trials-For-Womens-Gymnastics.

Todd, Carolyn L. "Here's What Might Have Caused Simone Biles' Dangerous 'Twisties' during the Tokyo Olympics." *Self*, September 27, 2021. https://www.self.com/story/simone-biles-twisties-anxiety -tokyo-olympics.

LEARN MORE

Fishman, Jon M. *Simone Biles, 2nd Edition.* Minneapolis: Lerner Publications, 2021.

Gold Over America Tour
https://www.goldoveramericatour.com/goat

Hewson, Anthony K. *Simone Biles.* Minneapolis: Abdo, 2022.

Morgan, Sally J. *Simone Biles: Golden Girl of Gymnastics.* New York: Random House Children's Books, 2020.

Olympics: Simone Biles
https://olympics.com/en/athletes/simone-biles

Simone Biles
https://simonebiles.com

INDEX